THE
GENDER
BOOK

from the author

The Pronoun Book
She, He, They, and Me!
Cassandra Jules Corrigan
Illustrated by Jem Milton
ISBN 978 1 78775 957 2
eISBN 978 1 78775 958 9

of related interest

Me and My Dysphoria Monster
An Empowering Story to Help Children Cope with Gender Dysphoria
Laura Kate Dale
Illustrated by Ang Hui Qing
ISBN 978 1 83997 092 4
eISBN 978 1 83997 093 1

Gender Heroes
25 Amazing Transgender, Non-Binary and Genderqueer Trailblazers from Past and Present!
Illustrated by Filipa Namorado
ISBN 978 1 83997 325 3
eISBN 978 1 83997 326 0

The Big Book of Pride Flags
Illustrated by Jem Milton
ISBN 978 1 83997 258 4
eISBN 978 1 83997 259 1

The GENDER BOOK

GIRLS, BOYS, NON-BINARY, AND BEYOND

Cassandra Jules Corrigan

Illustrated by Jem Milton

Jessica Kingsley Publishers
London and Philadelphia

First published in Great Britain in 2023 by Jessica Kingsley Publishers
An imprint of John Murray Press

1

A CIP catalogue record for this title is available from the British
Library and the Library of Congress

ISBN 978 1 83997 710 7
eISBN 978 1 83997 711 4

Printed and bound in China by Leo Paper Products Ltd

Jessica Kingsley Publishers' policy is to use papers that are natural,
renewable and recyclable products and made from wood grown in
sustainable forests. The logging and manufacturing processes are
expected to conform to the environmental regulations of the country
of origin.

Jessica Kingsley Publishers
Carmelite House
50 Victoria Embankment
London EC4Y 0DZ

www.jkp.com

John Murray Press
Part of Hodder & Stoughton Limited
An Hachette UK Company

To Sadie: Thank you for your help as a writer and a friend.

When each person is born, they're given an **assigned gender at birth** based on their perceived biological sex.

Generally, this gender will either be **male** or **female**, although you might also hear these genders referred to as **boy** and **girl**. These are called the **binary genders** because many people see them as opposites of one another.

Often someone who was assigned female at birth will refer to themselves as **AFAB** for short, and someone who was assigned male at birth might call themselves **AMAB**.

IT'S A BOY!

Whether someone is assigned male or female at birth is usually determined by their **chromosomes**. Chromosomes is a big word we use to describe a part of our DNA that makes us who we are.

Before we're born and still growing in our parent's belly, our chromosomes determine what kind of body we'll have.

Most people who are assigned male at birth have XY chromosomes, while most people who are assigned female at birth have XX chromosomes.

Every once in a while, someone is born who is not easily categorized as male or female. These people are called **intersex**.

Sometimes doctors can tell that a baby is intersex as soon as they are born, but other times people who are intersex are assigned male or female at birth and don't know they're intersex until much later in life. Some people don't even know they're intersex until they're grown up.

Some scientists think that intersex people could make up 1.7 percent of the population. For comparison, people with natural red hair make up only 1 to 2 percent of the population.

While 1.7 percent might not seem like a lot, that means that there are over 135 million intersex people around the world. Can you count that high?

In addition to an assigned gender at birth, we each have a **gender identity** and a **gender expression**.

A gender identity is the gender that most feels like ours. A gender expression is how we present our gender identity to the world.

Some people are **gender non-conforming,** which means they express their gender in a way that is different to how society expects them to.

Hi, my name is Tyshon and I identify as a man, but I have a feminine gender expression.

I like to wear make-up and have long hair like many women, but that doesn't make me any less of a man. I am gender non-conforming.

Hi, my name is Nina. My gender identity is female, but my gender expression is masculine. I'm gender non-conforming.

Often trans people experience **gender dysphoria**—they might feel upset because their assigned gender at birth doesn't match their gender identity.

Sometimes, in order to get rid of gender dysphoria, trans people change their names or appearances to better reflect their gender identities. This is called **transitioning**.

Some people transition **medically,** through taking medicine or having surgery. Other people transition **socially,** by changing their names, pronouns, or the way they dress. Some trans people don't transition at all.

Trans people may also experience **gender euphoria**, which is a feeling of joy as a result of being perceived as your true gender identity.

Finding your true gender identity is something to be celebrated. Some trans people even hold parties to announce their new genders, names, or pronouns to their loved ones.

IT'S A GIRL

Many trans people transition from one binary gender to the other. Other people don't feel like either binary gender fits them and identify with a **non-binary gender**.

Others are still questioning which gender is right for them, or don't identify as any gender. These people might call themselves **agender**, **greygender**, or prefer not to have any gender label at all.

There are many non-binary genders, so let's learn about a few of them together!

Hi, my name is Anteco. I identify as having no gender. I'm agender.

Hi, my name is Andrew. I was assigned male at birth, but I'm questioning if it's really my gender identity. In the meantime, I prefer not to use any label for my gender.

Hi, my name is Lisa. I know I'm non-binary, but I don't really have a more specific label for myself. Whenever someone asks me my gender, I just say I'm non-binary or greygender.

 Some people are neurodivergent, meaning that they have a condition such as autism or ADHD that makes them think about the world in a different way than those who don't share their medical condition.

Neurodivergence can make it difficult to explain your gender, so in 2014, neurodivergent people coined the word

GENDERVAGUE

to describe people who can't define their gender because of their neurodivergence or whose gender and neurodivergence are closely related.

Hi, I'm Sadie. I have DID, or dissociative identity disorder, which means I have multiple personality states called alters.
Not all of my alters are the same gender, so I prefer to call myself gendervague.
Hi, my name's Amanda, and I have ADHD. For a long time, it was very rare for people like me, who are assigned female at birth, to be diagnosed with ADHD.
When I got my diagnosis, I began to question if I was really a girl. I'm proud to be both AFAB and ADHD, but I now identify as gendervague.
Hi, my name is Cam. I have post-traumatic stress disorder related to my assigned gender at birth.
Identifying as gendervague makes me feel much safer and happier than I was before.

Some people feel like their identity can be best described by mixing labels.
For example, I identify as a female-aligned genderqueer person. Female-aligned and genderqueer are two separate identities, but I use them both to form a new identity that's all my own.
Wow! We've learned a lot today!
And when it comes to gender identity, there is always more to discover, because there are always more people in the world we haven't met yet.

That's right! Gender is a very personal thing because it's one part of the whole of what makes us who we are. So one person's definition and experience of being bigender could be very different from another bigender person's.
Think about it like eye color. Ellie and I both have brown eyes, but the shades of our eyes don't quite match. You will probably never meet someone with the exact same shade of eye color as you, and the same is true about gender identity.

Some girls cover their hair and that's an important part of how they understand their gender. Some boys wear skirts and that's one aspect of how they experience being boys.

Growing up, you may want to experiment with your assigned gender at birth and, in the process, you could find out that your assigned gender at birth isn't your true gender identity. Or you may find that your assigned gender at birth is the perfect fit for you.

Either way, we hope you know that there is a place for you, and remember that Ellie and I are so glad we've met you!

GLOSSARY OF TERMS

Autigender, adj.—a neurogender similar to gendervague, which is specific to autistic people.

Demiandrogyne, adj.—denoting someone who only partially relates to or identifies as androgyne.

Enby, n.—a non-binary person.

Femandrogyne, adj.—short for feminine androgyne, denoting an androgyne who feels more feminine than masculine.

Greygender, adj.—also known as grey-gender or grey agender, denoting someone who identifies as at least partially outside of the gender binary and who has ambivalence about their gender identity and gender expression.

Mascandrogyne, adj.—short for masculine androgyne, denoting an androgyne who feels more masculine than feminine.

Neurogender, n.—any gender that is connected to a person's neurodivergence (e.g. gendervague or autgender).

Neutrandrogyne, adj.—short for neutral androgyne, denoting an androgyne who might feel a relatively even mixture of femininity and masculinity, or even none at all.

Neutrois, adj.—denoting someone who identifies as a "neutral" or "null" gender.

Third Gender, adj.—denoting a person who is categorized as neither male or female, but as another gender entirely.

Transfeminine, adj.—denoting a person who was assigned male at birth but identifies as feminine.

Transmasculine, adj.—denoting a person who was assigned female at birth but identifies as masculine.

Two Spirit, adj.—a gender identity specific to Indigenous North Americans, which denotes that a person fulfils a traditional third gender role for their cultures.

Versandrogyne, adj.—short for versatile androgyne, denoting an androgyne whose amount of masculinity and femininity fluctuates.

GENDER COMPARISON ACTIVITY

 **1** Team up with one or more friends of the same gender.

2 Get pieces of paper and something to write with for each of you.

3 With your paper and pens, move to where you can't see each other's papers.

4 Spend a few minutes writing down things that you feel make you the gender you are or things you feel indicate to other people what gender you are. You might write down things like the way you dress, your favorite colors, how you act, or the kinds of games and toys you like to play with.

You might not feel like anything makes you one gender or another, and that's okay. You don't have to write down anything if you don't want to!

 **5** If you belong to one of the binary genders (e.g. boy or girl) make a separate list of things about you that are sometimes associated with the other binary gender. For example, if you're a boy, but you like to play with dolls, you might write that down. Ask yourself if these things make you feel any differently about your gender or if you see them as just another part of you.

Remember, these things don't make you any less of a boy or girl. This is just to get you thinking!

 **6** Once you and your friends are done writing, come back together and compare your lists. Do your lists match or are they different? Did this make you rethink what things are "for girls" or "for boys"?